"I'D LIKE TO BE A QUEEN OF PEOPLE'S HEARTS…"

—Princess Diana

Princess Diana in Ipswich, Suffolk, 1990.

The People's Princess

A MEMORIAL

STEWART, TABORI & CHANG
NEW YORK

Edited by Katrina and Natasha Fried

Photo captions by H.D.R. Campbell

Publisher: Lena Tabori
Art Director: J. C. Suarès
Designer: Lisa Vaughn
Production: Amanda Freymann

Published in 1997 and distributed in the U.S. by
Stewart, Tabori & Chang,
a division of U.S. Media Holdings, Inc.
115 West 18th Street, New York, NY 10011

Distributed in Canada by
General Publishing Company Ltd.
30 Lesmill Road
Don Mills, Ontario, Canada M3B 2T6

Sold in Australia by
Peribo Pty Ltd.
58 Beaumont Road
Mount Kuring-gai, NSW 2080, Australia

Distributed in all other territories by
Grantham Book Services Ltd.
Isaac Newton Way, Alma Park Industrial Estate
Grantham, Lincolnshire, NG31 9SD, England

Library of Congress Catalog Card Number: 97-62004

Collector's First Edition - First printing 50,000

Printed in the United States of America

10 9 8 7 6 5 4 3 2 1

DIANA WITH HARRY AND WILLIAM, MARJORCA, SPAIN, 1987.

LADY DIANA SPENCER WITH HER YOUNGER BROTHER, CHARLES, AT PARK HOUSE,
SANDRINGHAM, NORFOLK, 1967.

Earl Charles Spencer's Eulogy
September 6, 1997

stand before you today the representative of a family in grief in a country in mourning before a world in shock. We are all united, not only in our desire to pay our respects to Diana, but rather in our need to do so. For such was her extraordinary appeal that the tens of millions of people taking part in this service all over the world, via television and radio, who never actually met her, feel that they too lost someone close to them in the early hours of Sunday morning. It is a more remarkable tribute to Diana than I can ever hope to offer her today.

Diana was the very essence of compassion, of duty, of style, of beauty. All over the world she was the symbol of selfless humanity, a standard bearer for the rights of the truly downtrodden, a very British girl who transcended nationality, someone with a natural nobility, who was classless, and who proved in the last year that she needed no royal title to continue to generate her particular brand of magic.

Today is our chance to say thank you to the way you brightened our lives, even though God granted you but half a life. We will all feel cheated always that you were taken from us so young, and yet we must learn to be grateful that you came along at all. Only now that you are gone do we truly appreciate what we are now without, and we want you to know that life without you is very, very difficult. We have all despaired at our loss over the past week, and only the strength of the message you gave us through your years of giving has afforded us the strength to move forward.

There is a temptation to rush to canonize your memory; there is no need to do so. You stand tall enough as a human being of unique qualities; you do not need to be seen as a saint. Indeed, to sanctify your memory would be to miss out on the very core of your being: your wonderfully mischievous sense of humor with a laugh that bent you double, your joy for life transmitted wherever you took your smile and the sparkle in those unforgettable eyes, your boundless energy which you could barely contain. But your greatest gift was your intuition, and it was a gift you used wisely. This is what underpinned all your other wonderful attributes, and if we look to analyse what it was about you that had such a wide appeal we find it in your instinctive feel for what was really important in all our lives.

Without your God-given sensitivity we would be immersed in greater ignorance at the anguish of AIDS and HIV sufferers, the plight of the homeless, the isolation of lepers, the random destruction of landmines. Diana explained to me once that it was her innermost feelings of suffering that made it possible for her to connect with her constituency of the rejected. And here we come to another truth about her: for all the status, the glamour, the applause, Diana remained, throughout, a very insecure person at heart, almost childlike in her desire to do good for others, so she could release herself from deep feelings of unworthiness, of which her eating disorders were merely a symptom. The world sensed this part of her character and cherished her for her vulnerability whilst admiring her for her honesty.

The last time I saw Diana was on July the first, her birthday, in London when, typically, she was not taking time to celebrate her special day with friends, but was guest of honor at a fundraising charity that evening. She sparkled of course, but I would rather cherish the days I spent with her in March when she came to visit me and my children at our home in South Africa. I am proud of the fact that apart from when she was on public display meeting President Mandela, we managed to contrive to stop the ever-present paparazzi from getting a single picture of her. That meant a lot to her. These were days I will always treasure. It was as if we had been transported back to our childhood when we spent such an enormous amount of time together, the two youngest in the family. Fundamentally, she hadn't changed at all from the big sister who mothered me as a baby, fought with me at school, and endured those long train journeys between our parents' homes with me at weekends. It is a tribute to her level headedness and strength that despite the most bizarre life imaginable after her childhood she remained intact, true to herself.

There is no doubt that she was looking for new direction in her life at this time. She talked endlessly of getting away from England, mainly because of the treatment that she received at the hands of the newspapers. I don't think she ever understood why her genuinely good intentions were sneered at by the media, why there appeared to be a permanent quest on their behalf to bring her down. It is baffling. My own and only explanation is that genuine goodness is threatening to those at the opposite end of the moral spectrum. It is a point to remember that of all the ironies about Diana, perhaps the greatest was this: A girl given the name of the ancient goddess of hunting was, in the end, the most hunted person of the modern age.

She would want us today to pledge ourselves to protecting her beloved boys, William and Harry, from a similar fate, and I do this here Diana, on your behalf. We will not allow them to suffer the anguish that used regularly to drive you to tearful despair. And beyond that, on behalf of your mother and sisters, I pledge that we, your blood family, will do all we can to continue the imaginative and loving way you were steering these exceptional young men, so that their souls are not simply immersed by duty and tradition, but can sing openly as you planned. We fully respect the heritage into which they have both been born and will always respect and encourage them in their royal role. But we, like you, recognize the need for them to experience as many different aspects to life as possible, to arm them spiritually and emotionally for the years ahead. I know you would have expected nothing less from us.

William and Harry, we all care desperately for you today. We are all chewed up with sadness at the loss of a woman who wasn't even our mother. How great your suffering is we cannot even imagine.

I would like to end by thanking God for the small mercies he's shown us this dreadful time, for taking Diana at her most beautiful and radiant when she had joy in her private life. Above all we give thanks for the life of a woman I am so proud to be able to call my sister, the unique, the complex, the extraordinary and irreplaceable Diana whose beauty, both internal and external, will never be extinguished from our minds.

A PORTRAIT OF THE PRINCESS OF WALES COMMISSIONED BY VOGUE MAGAZINE FOR ITS DECEMBER 1990 ISSUE.

I remember thinking what a very jolly and amusing and attractive sixteen-year-old she was, and I mean great fun and bouncy and full of life and everything. And I don't know what she thought of me.

—Prince Charles, 1981

CHARLES AND DIANA AT BALMORAL, SCOTLAND, 1981,
TWO MONTHS PRIOR TO THEIR WEDDING.

FROM THE PHOTOGRAPHY SESSION ON THEIR WEDDING DAY, JULY 29, 1981, AT
BUCKINGHAM PALACE. (OVERLEAF)

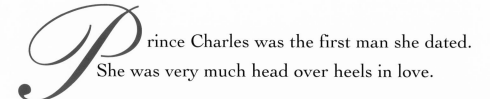

*P*rince Charles was the first man she dated. She was very much head over heels in love.

—Harry Herbert, whose father manages the Queen's stables and who, as a teenager, spent time with the young Diana

DIANA AND CHARLES AFTER A WINDSOR POLO MATCH IN 1987.

*Y*ou didn't feel she was English royalty as much as she was a person—this youthful, independent, courageous woman. She just seemed like one of us.

—Mary Holden, Black Mountain, North Carolina

LADY DIANA SPENCER IN AN EARLY PUBLIC APPEARANCE IN THE VILLAGE OF TETBURY
PRIOR TO HER 1981 WEDDING TO PRINCE CHARLES.

CHARLES AND DIANA VISIT THE ITALIAN NAVAL BASE OF LA SPEZIA, 1985.

*T*think, like any marriage, especially when you've had divorced parents, like myself, you'd want to try even harder to make it work, and you don't want to fall back into a pattern that you've seen happen in your own family. I desperately wanted it to work. I desperately loved my husband, and I wanted to share everything together. I thought that we were a very good team…Here was a fairy story that everybody wanted to work. And it was isolating, but it was also a situation where you couldn't indulge in feeling sorry for yourself. You had to either sink or swim, and you had to learn that very fast…I swam.

—Princess Diana, 1995

DIANA DISCHARGING HER ROYAL DUTIES, 1989. (LEFT)

DIANA AND CHARLES ON A VISIT TO A CHATEAU IN FRANCE, 1988. (ABOVE)

*S*he stooped to talk gently with children, touched the blind, and embraced the elderly, dazzling the cameras with a demure but seductive smile that found its way onto every front page.

—Jonathan Dimbleby, in his biography of
Prince Charles, The Prince of Wales

DIANA VISITS HER OWN REGIMENT, THE PRINCESS OF WALES HOME BARRACKS, CANTERBURY, 1995.

DIANA WITH THE ROYAL HAMPSHIRE REGIMENT, WEST BERLIN, 1985.

*N*o one can tell me how to behave. I work by instinct. That's my best adviser.

—Princess Diana, June 1997

She was very quick and very funny. I remember one time she was flying on Virgin Atlantic and she swapped clothing with a stewardess. And as we were crossing over Windsor Castle, she got on the cabin speaker, telling the passengers, "If you'll look out your right-hand window, you'll see Granny's place."

—Richard Branson

CHARLES PROVES TO BE A GOOD SPORT AS DIANA SMASHES A BREAKAWAY CHAMPAGNE BOTTLE ON HIS HEAD ON A LONDON MOVIE SET, 1990. (OVERLEAF)

THE PRINCESS AT A BENEFIT IN NEW YORK CITY, DECEMBER 1995. (ABOVE)

DIANA EXPERIMENTED WITH POLKA DOTS IN HER WARDROBE INCLUDING SOCKS,
TROUSERS, HATS, SHOES, AND DRESSES, 1987. (LEFT)

One of my favorite memories of Diana was being with her children. I visited them several times at Kensington and once took a needlepoint rocker chair to young Prince William. Like most small boys, he seemed more fascinated with the box it came in than the gift itself. What is it about boxes and small boys? I remember William playing under the stairwell, and he seemed to want me to join him, so I took off my shoes and we had a wonderful time playing together. I know everyone talks about the problem in the Waleses' marriage, but I remember their home being very warm. Those boys are Diana's greatest legacy.

—*Nancy Reagan*

PRINCESS DIANA WITH HER FIRST BORN, PRINCE WILLIAM, AT THE WIMBLEDON WOMEN'S FINAL, 1991.

I want to bring them up with security. I hug my children to death and get into bed with them at night. I always feed them love and affection; it's so important.

—Princess Diana

PRINCESS DIANA WITH HER YOUNGER SON, HARRY, ON HOLIDAY IN
MAJORCA, SPAIN, 1987.

DIANA WITH HARRY IN MARJORCA, SPAIN, 1986. (ABOVE)

DIANA AND CHARLES LEAVE ST. MARY'S HOSPITAL IN SEPTEMBER 1984 WITH THEIR
NEWBORN SON, PRINCE HARRY. (RIGHT)

THE PRINCESS WITH HER SONS, PRINCES HARRY AND WILLIAM, AT ETON COLLEGE, 1995. (ABOVE)

TROOPING THE COLOUR IN LONDON WITH THE QUEEN MOTHER AND PRINCE HARRY, 1989. (OVERLEAF)

*T*mean, once or twice I've had people say to me that, you know, that Diana's out to destroy the monarchy, which bewilders me, because why would I want to destroy something that is my children's future? I will fight for my children on any level in order for them to be happy and have peace of mind and carry out their duties.

I've taken them round to homelessness projects. I've taken William and Harry to people dying of AIDS, albeit I told them it was cancer. I want them to have an understanding of people's emotions, people's insecurities, people's distress, and people's hopes and dreams.

—Princess Diana

She was straightforward. When we walked into the shelter she turned around and she says, "Tonight I'm not a princess, my sons are not the two princes." She says, "I'm Diana, this is William and this is Harry." It will always remain in my memories. Diana said to me "You never look up, you never look down, you look straight ahead."

—a homeless man

*S*he was the people's princess and that is how she will stay, how she will remain, in our hearts and our memories forever…The whole of our country, all of us, will be in a state of mourning. Diana was a wonderful, warm and compassionate person who people, not just in Britain, but throughout the world loved and will be mourned as a friend.

How many times shall we remember her in how many different ways with the sick, the dying, with children, with the needy? When with just a look or a gesture that spoke so much more than words she would reveal to all of us the depth of her compassion and of her humanity.

The world has lost a princess who is simply irreplaceable.

—British Prime Minister Tony Blair

THE PRINCESS OF WALES SURROUNDED BY A SEA OF WAVING UNION JACKS.

PRINCESS DIANA MEETS WITH HIV SUFFERER, WILLIAM DRAKE, IN LONDON, 1992.

With one royal handshake given to a young man with AIDS in the late 1980s, Diana forever changed the face of AIDS for the world.

Here was the world's most famous woman embracing AIDS with one simple act…and with that handshake, she educated the world about compassion, love, and understanding.

Diana will be sorely missed.

—David Harvey, executive director of
AIDS Policy Center for Children, Youth, and Families

She used to pop in at the middle of the night to see who else couldn't sleep at 2AM. There were lots of visits like that.

—Paul Theobold,
a resident at the AIDS center London Lighthouse

*S*he helped me to help the poor and that's the most beautiful thing. She was very much concerned about the poor, and her attitude towards the poor was good. That's why she came close to me.

—Mother Teresa

Mother Teresa and Diana in the South Bronx, New York at the Sisters of Mercy Church, 1997.

*B*eing permanently in the public eye gives me a special responsibility—to use the impact of photographs to get a message across, to make the world aware of an important cause, to stand up for certain values.

—*Princess Diana, June 1997*

DIANA VISITS THE SHRI SWAMINARAYAN MANDIR HINDU MISSION
AT HEASDEN, 1997.

She was the bare-shouldered beauty,
but she was also Peter Pan's Wendy, ministering
to an entire nation of Lost Boys.

—Simon Schama

DIANA ATTENDS AN OFFICIAL BANQUET IN RIO DE JANEIRO, BRAZIL, 1991.

*I*f I should die and leave you here awhile, but not like others, sad undone, who keep long vigils by the silent dust and weep.

For my sake, turn again to life and smile, knowing thy heart and trembling hand to do something to comfort other hearts than thine.

Complete these dear and unfinished tasks of mine, and I, perchance, may therein comfort you.

—*Mary Lee Hall,* Turn Again to Life, *read by Sarah McCorquodale, Princess Diana's sister, at the funeral*

DIANA IN MODEST ATTIRE AT A DESERT PICNIC DURING A TRIP TO ABU DHABI, 1989.

n her life, Diana profoundly influenced this nation and the world. Although a princess, she was someone for whom from afar we dared to feel affection and by whom we were all intrigued. She kept company with kings and queens, with princes and with presidents, but especially we remember her humane concerns and how she met individuals and made them feel significant.

— The Reverend Dr. Wesley Carr

THE PRINCESS MEETS THE CHILDREN AT GARRAHAN HOSPITAL IN ARGENTINA, 1995.

*S*he made errors and she had weaknesses
every woman understands.

—*Lynn-Marie Williams,*
a thirty-three-year-old elementary school teacher

THE NEWLYWEDS ATTEND THE BRAEMAR HIGHLAND GAMES IN SCOTLAND,
SEPTEMBER, 1981.

*Y*ou think you are not addicted to her, but all of a sudden she is taken away from you and you realize that, unwillingly, you are.

—mourner

THE PRINCESS OF WALES IN LONDON ON THE OCCASION OF THE QUEEN MOTHER'S EIGHTY-SEVENTH BIRTHDAY, 1987.

*T*hought she'd come in with loads of security guards and an entourage like a rock star maybe would…but the door burst open and this physically beautiful and radiant creature in a red-and-white striped miniskirt and a red jacket and lovely delicate jewelry… soaking wet with her hair plastered down across her face, a bit of underskirt showing, slightly out of breath from running upstairs, said, "Hi! You must be Philip, you must be Julie. Louise, it's wonderful to see you, please sit down. I'm sorry. I must look like a drowned rat." Louise always said it was the proudest day of her life.

—Philip and Julie Woolcock, whose dying daughter, Louise , was visited by Princess Diana shortly before her death.

VISITING WEST BERLIN, DIANA SPARKLES WHILE CHARLES LISTENS, 1987.

THE PRINCESS OF WALES IN THE AUSTRALIAN OUTBACK TOWN OF
ALICE SPRINGS, 1983.

Princess Diana at a regiment review in Hyde Park, 1989.

THE PRINCESS OF WALES ON A SKIING HOLIDAY IN 1985.

AT THE BURGHLEY HORSE TRIALS, DIANA SMILES, 1989.

If you spent time with her, you felt Diana's extraordinary strength, as well as her vulnerability and her somewhat mocking and ever-present humor. I asked her if she had ever thought of going to college now that she was alone. She found my question hard to believe and commented with irony: "I've already had an education." She was right. Even though she lacked degrees, she had had a long, excruciating experience.

She seemed to have a clear determination to be her own person. Someone once asked her if she gambled. "Not with cards," she replied, "but with life."

—*Katharine Graham*

DIANA WORE THIS COAT DRESS OFTEN, VARYING THE LOOK BY CHANGING HATS, 1982.

*T*think I'll say to my daughters…that princesses are real. There was one once who was quite something.

—Jerry White, who along with his partner in the Landmine Survivor Network, took Princess Diana to meet with landmine survivors in Bosnia

THE PRINCESS OF WALES COMFORTS LANDMINE VICTIMS IN BOSNIA, 1997.

DIANA TRAVELS TO ANGOLA TO TOUR RED CROSS DE-MINING AREAS, 1997.

*S*he wanted to know everything. How I survived, how my wife helped me survive, how we have coped with it. At first I was paralyzed—it was a big thing to have a princess in your home. But after a while, I felt as if we had known each other for a long time. She wanted to see my stumps, she looked into my eyes. I couldn't see her clearly, but it's much more telling what one feels than what one sees.

—Franjo Kresic, who lost both legs and had his eyesight damaged by landmines in Bosnia

ime is too slow for those who wait,

too swift for those who fear,

too long for those who grieve,

too short for those who rejoice.

But for those who love, time is eternity.

—*David LaFlamme*, Time Is, *read by Lady Jane Fellowes,*
Princess Diana's sister, at the funeral

PRINCESS DIANA AND HARRY AT HIGHGROVE, 1990.

PRINCESS DIANA AND QUEEN ELIZABETH II ON THEIR WAY TO THE OPENING OF
PARLIAMENT, 1982.

*S*o what I say to you now as your Queen and as a grandmother, I say from my heart.

First, I want to pay tribute to Diana myself. She was an exceptional and gifted human being. In good times and bad, she never lost her capacity to smile and laugh, nor to inspire others with her warmth and kindness. I admired and respected her for her energy and commitment to others, and especially for her devotion to her two boys. This week at Balmoral we have all been trying to help William and Harry come to terms with the devastating loss that they and the rest of us have suffered.

No one who knew Diana will ever forget her.

—*Queen Elizabeth*

THE ROYAL FAMILY GATHERS ON THE BALCONY AT BUCKINGHAM PALACE FOR THE TROOPING OF THE COLOUR, 1989. (OVERLEAF)

*A*s a friend she was steadfast and loyal.
She did everything from the heart.
Her heart ruled her head is why,
I think, she was so often misunderstood.

—*Rosa Monckton*

DIANA APPEARS IN BARRA, THE SCOTTISH WESTERN ISLES,
IN SPITE OF A RAINSTORM, 1985.

She brings oxygen into the room.

—Marguerite Littman, founder of the AIDS Crisis Trust.

AT HER PUBLIC WALKABOUTS, THE PRINCESS GRAVITATED TOWARDS THE CHILDREN,
SWANSEA, 1992.

You know I met her really at the beginning, when she was married with Prince Charles, and of course I immediately realized she was one of really the most beautiful girls in the world. Finally, year by year she became more sophisticated and more sure of herself. She was full of guts, full of elegance. And every designer was inspired by her. I did have the chance and the honor to make several dresses for her. To me she will remain one of the most beautiful darling ladies in the world.

— Valentino

PRINCESS DIANA, A PATRON OF THE SERPENTINE GALLERY IN LONDON,
ARRIVES FOR A GALA EVENING, 1994

EXTREMELY FIT, THE PRINCESS CUTS AN ENVIABLE FIGURE.

*E*ven among models, there are no legs like this.

—Karl Lagerfeld

I was told the White House party was one of the biggest nights of her life. To say that I was honored would be an understatement because it was one of the biggest nights of my life. Nancy had asked me if I would please dance with Diana because it was her big wish. So I went and asked her, and she blushed. We danced for about ten minutes, every song from the old movies that I'd done. The floor cleared. It was like a fairy tale.

—John Travolta

PRINCESS DIANA DANCES WITH JOHN TRAVOLTA AT THE WHITE HOUSE, WASHINGTON, D.C., 1985. (OVERLEAF)

There she was, right in front of me, and I instantly realized that no kind of film, whether still or moving, had done her justice. She wasn't just beautiful. She was like the sun coming up: coming up giggling.

—Clive James

EVEN AT THE HEIGHT OF HER PHYSICAL AILMENTS, DIANA APPEARED HAPPY AND BEAUTIFUL.

*T*hank God for the gift of Diana and for all her loving and giving. I give her back to Him, with my love, pride, and admiration, to rest in peace.

—Frances Shand Kydd, Diana's mother

DIANA ON AN OFFICIAL STATE VISIT IN SYDNEY, AUSTRALIA FOR THE BICENTENNIAL, 1988.

THE PEOPLE'S PRINCESS

90

DIANA RIVER RAFTING WITH HER SONS, WILLIAM AND HARRY IN ASPEN, COLORADO, 1992.

At Thorpe Park in 1992, Diana takes a soaking with her son,
Prince Harry. (above)

Racing at the annual sports day at Wetherby, Prince William's London
school, Diana takes second place in the eighty-yard sprint, 1989. (overleaf)

PHOTO CREDITS